A Handbook for

DEMOLITION AND CLEARANCE CREWS

Prepared by the Training Section

U. S. OFFICE OF CIVILIAN DEFENSE

U. S. Government Printing Office, December 1941, Wash., D. C.

PREFACE

This is one of a series of civilian defense handbooks prepared by the United States Office of Civilian Defense. The purpose of each handbook is to instruct the individual enrolled civilian defense worker in his duties, and to serve as a manual for reference.

The measures for safeguarding civilians against the effects of air attack, which are described in the following pages, have become a necessary part of the defensive organization of any country open to air attack.

Every State and municipality should take such legal or administrative action as may be necessary to provide for the organization, direction, and training of its Demolition and Clearance Crews.

F. H. LaGuardia,
U. S. Director Civilian Defense.

Washington, D. C.
December 1941

CONTENTS

	Page
Chain of Command	1
Number of Volunteer Demolition and Clearance Crews	1
Headquarters for Demolition and Clearance Crews	2
Duties	3
Training Requirements	3
Trucks, Cars	4
Equipping the Truck or Car	4
Other Machinery — Tractors, Bulldozers, Etc.	5
Duties Preliminary to An Air Attack	7
Delayed-Action Bombs	7
After the Raid	8
Acetylene Torches	9
Explosives	10
Using Tools and Equipment	10
Standard Symbols for Maps	11
Types of Direction Signs	12
Notes	12-13
Blackouts	15
Warning System	18
What to do In an Air Raid	20
Fire Defense	21
Magnesium Bomb	22
Water Control of Incendiaries	23
Sand Control of Incendiaries	24
Fire Extinguishers	25
Chemical Warfare Agents, Chart	26
War Gases	27
Gas-tight Room	28
Decontamination	29
Citizens' Defense Corps	31
Enrolled Services, C. D. C.	31
Drill Manual, C. D. C.	33

III

DEMOLITION AND CLEARANCE CREWS

Chain of Command.

In the local organization of Civilian Defense, the Demolition and Clearance Crews are usually under the supervision of the Public Works Emergency Division Chief. In communities where a Department of Public Works does not exist an organization should be set up to operate, under one head: The Demolition and Clearance Crews, the Road Repair Crews, and the Decontamination Squads.

These three services work together at all times and operate best under one head, however, each may be organized, trained, equipped, and supervised separately.

Number of Volunteer Demolition and Clearance Crews.

Demolition and Clearance Crews each consisting of 8 to 12 men are organized for each 4,000 to 5,000 population. These crews are further organized into Truck Companies which consist of two or more crews. In communities of 100,000 or less all truck companies are under the supervision of the Public Works Emergency Division

Chief. In larger communities an assistant may be appointed by the chief, for each 100,000 population. Truck company leaders are appointed by the Public Works Emergency Division Chief or by his assistant. Crew leaders are appointed by truck company leaders.

Truck Companies may not always be organized alike. If necessary several companies will be grouped in order that the following combinations may be affected:

Light

Superintendent and Blaster.
Assistant Superintendent–Torch Operator.
Electric and Gas Experts (2).
Riggers (4).
Laborers (High Men) (6).
Laborers (Ground) (10).

Heavy

Superintendent and Blaster.
Assistant Superintendent–Torch Operator.
Riggers (4).
Equipment Operators.
Laborers (High Men) (15).
Laborers (Ground) (20).
Dynamite Man.
Cutting Torch Operator.
Electrical and Gas Experts (4).

These combinations are only possible in the larger cities. In the smaller communities, companies will be organized in a manner suitable to the tasks with which they will have to deal.

Headquarters for Demolition and Clearance Crews.

Truck Companies with their trucks and equipment will be stationed at strategic points throughout the community where facilities for repair and servicing can be secured. Truck Companies should not be quartered close to prominent buildings or oil storage tanks that may be the object of a raid.

Duties.

You have been selected as a member of a Demolition and Clearance Crew because you are husky, able to work hard long hours in all kinds of weather, possess unusual mental attributes to quickly size up a job and are amenable to discipline.

Each problem will present a new experience to most of you. The tools on hand plus those that can be made available to you on short notice must be put to their best use. Walls should be pulled down or dynamited wherever they are a hazard to life. Craters should be filled in and roads cleared. Rubble will be removed as quickly as possible. Where power shovels or scrapers are not available, hand shovels must be used.

Training Requirements.

Each member of a Demolition and Clearance Crew is required to be proficient in the following subjects:

1. Fire Defense—3 Hours.
2. Gas Defense—2 Hours.
3. General Course—5 Hours.
4. Drill—2 Hours.
5. Special Course—You will be given special instructions by contractors and engineers, who, from their personal experience will be able to pass on to you many valuable tips.

Leaders will be specialists and will not ask you to perform any job beyond your ability. It is not anticipated that you will be required to take unnecessary risks. Projects that are beyond the skill of Local Demolition and Clearance Crews ability will be abandoned until trained personnel can be secured.

Trucks, Cars.

It is doubtful if there are very many municipalities that can set aside vehicles equipped to be used for air raid work alone. However, dependable vehicles should be made available and reserve quantities of oil and gasoline stored for emergency use. There will be a driver and an Assistant Driver appointed by the Truck Company Leader for each vehicle.

Equipping the Truck or Car.

In most cases it will be necessary to obtain Demolition and Clearance equipment by purchase or by loan. This should be stored close to the truck and a supply of fuel and repair parts be made a part of the service load.

Suggested Equipment:

Hand truck complete with acetylene tanks, hose, torches, wrenches, striker. (Tent secured to back) goggles.

Shovels, round end.
Shovels, square end.
Shoring poles.
Picks.
Mattocks.
Crowbars, long.
Wrecking bars.

Pinch bars.
Axes.
Rope, 1½", 500 ft.
Cable, 1" steel, 200 ft.
Sledge hammer, 10–12 lb.
Wheelbarrows.
Dynamite.
Rope, ½" and signs to rope off danger area.
Ladders—various.
Detonator.
Dynamite caps.
Heavy work gloves.
Gloves, rubber.
Set of rope tackle, 3 sheave.
Single sheave snatch block
Jacks (2) 10–15 ton lift.
Crosscut saws. 2-handled.
Box of miscellaneous tools, spikes, wedges, etc.
Tools to shut off gas and water at curb or meter.
Electric cable.
Lamps, 250–500 watts.
Saws—carpenters, hack, cross-cut.

The amount of equipment allocated for Demolition and Clearance Crews should be based on the probable needs of the community.

Other Machinery—Tractors, Bulldozers, Etc.

A tractor with a scraping attachment or a bulldozer is almost indispensable for cleaning up debris and should be available in every community.

For fast transportation a truck with a ramp will speed up delivery of slow-moving equipment to the scene of an incident.

Cities that are able to provide all this equipment will be the exception rather than the rule. It is not anticipated that every community will

at once purchase everything that might be needed, however, every attempt should be made to secure a good supply of the simpler tools that will do the job efficiently by substituting hand power for mechanical horsepower.

Vehicles when available:
>   Truck with winch and searchlight (2-ton).
>   Crew trucks 2½-ton.
>   Dump trucks, 1½-ton.
>   Motor-truck cranes.

Duties Preliminary to An Air Attack.

After your crew and truck company is organized it will be necessary for you to study the various systems for providing water, gas, and electricity and methods of cutting off these utilities in buildings to be demolished. Call on the Utilities Repair Squads if time permits.

Vehicles should be kept loaded at all times except when they are used for other purposes. Have a place for everything and keep everything in its place. Practice loading vehicles and answering calls.

Delayed-Action Bombs.

Bombs, other than incendiary bombs, that fall near where you are working will be reported to the nearest Air Raid Warden at once. When they fail to explode, if your crew is working within the danger area, work will be stopped at once and the crew and equipment withdrawn to a safe distance.

After the Raid.

Your truck company will be assigned certain specific sections to clean up. Upon receipt of orders you will proceed to that section, with all your equipment and prepare to raze any structures found to be in precarious condition.

After certain information is secured from the Warden-in-Charge, that there are no living or dead in any part of the buildings to be razed, the water, gas, and electric services will be cut off, if possible, and the work begun.

Sections of wooden or frame homes and buildings should be wrecked toward the area formerly occupied by the structure. Brick buildings should be wrecked toward the area formerly occupied by the structure unless there is a demand for brick to fill in holes in the vicinity, then they will be wrecked toward the street or road where the rubble can be easily handled. Fallen parts of buildings will be kept from obstructing walks and streets as much as possible. Brick, stone, and lumber may be cleared from the adjoining walks and streets by scraper, power shovel, or by hand.

Care should be taken not to fill in any holes if there are broken mains or cables. Traffic should be detoured around such holes until repairs are completed by the Utilities Repair Squads.

Steel girders should be removed in one piece if possible. Acetylene cutting will only be resorted to when it is certain that there is no other alternative. Sections will be cut as long as is consistent with easy handling and conservation of material.

Multistoried buildings hit by high explosive bombs may be saved in part. It may be possible to remove one or more top floors and leave the remainder intact. Unless there is an extensive area beside the building where materials can be dropped, the damaged materials should be razed on the structure itself and then removed by the building elevator or an improvised elevator or chute. Care must be taken not to overload floors. Fissures in walls must be carefully inspected to determine whether parts of buildings can be saved.

Trucks and cars smashed by falling buildings should be removed with the least possible additional damage. Rubble should be removed from them by hand. If they will not start or move under their own power they should be hauled away.

Animals killed or injured by debris should be removed as soon as possible from the populated section and turned over to those experienced in their disposal.

Should you encounter gas, work will immediately be stopped. If there is no further work for you in the vicinity your headquarters should be contacted to ascertain if there is work elsewhere.

Acetylene Torches.

When possible acetylene torches should be available to Demolition and Clearance Squads. Fallen girders and beams will constitute a barrier to work. These will have to be cut or a great deal of time spent in detaching or removing entire sections of metal. A vehicle of some sort, capable of being wheeled into difficult places should be devised to transport tanks, hose, and torches. A sufficient supply of gas should be kept on hand to meet emergencies.

Metal cutting torches, in the hands of experts of the Demolition and Clearance Squads, can assist the fire fighting and rescue teams materially. Care should be exercised to prevent the starting of fires during cutting operations and not to place tanks where they will be crushed by falling walls or come in contact with high temperatures. Tanks have been known to explode with the force of a bomb. DO NOT USE ACETYLENE WHERE OIL IN ANY FORM IS PRESENT.

No attempt should be made to cut girders and beams to any size other than that necessary for easy loading and disposal.

Explosives.

Explosives will be handled by experienced blasters only. If one is not available the work will be accomplished in some other manner or the work will be abandoned, the area evacuated, roped off, and guards posted.

Using Tools and Equipment.

All equipment, chisels to motor cars, perform best through long and hard usage when properly conditioned. During periods of operation and while waiting for calls, no opportunity should be passed up to recondition and tune up equipment.

As some machinery is equipped with steel wheels, care will be exercised not to let them come in contact with power lines that might be down. Serious and fatal burns and shocks are frequently caused by neglecting this precaution.

Standard Symbols for Maps.

Use these standard symbols on all maps—they are intended to make clear the facts you and others will need to know in a hurry.

///.	Warden's Post	☼	Bomb Crater
ψ	Fire Watcher's Station	[ ]	Roped-off Area
↓ψ	Fire Alarm	┼┼┼┼	Street Car Tracks
☎	Telephone	╫╫╫	Double Tracks
δ	Air Raid Shelter	●	Cisterns or Water Reserves
G δ	Gas-Proof Air Raid Shelter	—¦—¦—¦	Sector Limits
IN▸	Entrance to Shelter	—‖—‖—	Zone Limits
♀	Fire Station	🛇	Site of Gas Bomb
◯	Decontamination Squad Depot	❀	Contaminated Area (For large area, blue cross-hatch)
R	Repair Squad	⊕	Street Lamp
✚	Casualty Station	🜛	Fire Hydrant
⨍	Decontaminating First Aid Station	‖‖‖‖‖	Sewer Gratings
⊥	Bomb Squad Station	⊛	Manhole
☐	Location of Incident (Show number in center)	♣	Tree
X	Demolished Building	🝆	Sandbags

11

Types of Direction Signs.

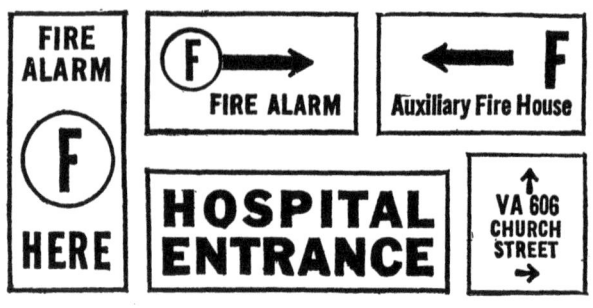

This Page is for Notes

This Page is for Notes

This Page is for Notes

This Page is for Notes

This Page is for Notes

This Page is for Notes

This Page is for Notes

This Page is for Notes

This Book Belongs to:

(First name)   (Initial)   (Last name)

My Home Address Is:

My Telephone Number Is:

----

or

My Home Can Be Reached by calling ----------

Demolition and Clearance Crew No. ----------

Truck Company No. ----------

In case of emergency, notify:

City ---------------------- *State* ----------------------

BLACKOUTS

Blackouts are ordered only on the authority of the War Department. A blackout may be ordered during any period when hostile forces are believed to be in the vicinity, whether or not enemy airplanes have been sighted.

"Blacking Out" a city means that light sources must be so hidden or dimmed that an enemy bomber will have difficulty in finding the target and lack aiming points such as main street intersections. Following are the general plans used.

Street Lights. These are fitted with low-watt bulbs and covers that diffuse the light.

Automobiles. Headlights must be covered except for a small pair of slits and hooded.

Traffic Lights. Are treated the same way as automobile headlights.

Buildings. Windows and doors must be covered with opaque materials. Paint on the glass, heavy curtains, light "baffles" or screens are some of the ways. No cracks of light must show.

Aids to Seeing. Since people have to move about during a blackout, the lack of light may be somewhat offset and safety promoted by—

1. Painting curbs, trees, poles and hydrants with white paint. There is a luminous paint, also, that gives off a faint blue light quite visible in total darkness.

2. Painting signs of luminous paint or making them of fluorescent material on which shines ultraviolet or "black" light or installing dimly lighted signs with horizontal screens to diffuse the light.

3. Painting white fenders and stripes around automobiles.

Members of the Citizens' Defense Corps who have outside duties during a blackout can be identified more easily if they wear a white cap or white-painted helmet; also a white belt fitted with crossed straps over the shoulders.

Individual Conduct During a Blackout.

Observe traffic rules. Keep to the right and remember the man or vehicle approaching *from* your right *has* the right of way.

If you must smoke, go into a hallway or covered place to strike the match. No smoking in the open is an even better rule. Make all crossings at intersections. It is hard for a driver to see you.

Be sure that everyone you know is acquainted with these simple rules.

DO NOT run when air raid warnings sound after dark during blackouts.

Use your flashlight as little as possible, if at all. Never point it upward.

Curb edges and direction signs painted white will help you find your way.

Keep pets on leash if you take them out after dark.

If an air raid warning sounds, get under cover, you may be hit by shell fragments.

If you don't know the neighborhood the first policeman or warden will tell you where to go.

When an observer sights a group of hostile planes, he picks up his telephone (1) and says *Army Flash*. The Central Operator (2) at once connects him with the assigned Filter Center (3) to which he reports the type of planes, number, height, and direction of flight. When several reports agree, watchers transmit the data to an Information Center (4) where developments over a large area are plotted on a huge map.

Watching the map, Air Corps officers order interceptor planes into the air, (5) direct them to contact with the enemy; another officer notes the cities threatened and flashes a yellow, blue, or red alarm, according to the degree of danger, to the proper Warning District Center (6).

At this point, Civilian Defense takes over from the Air Corps, telephones the warnings to Control Centers (7) within the Warning District. And here the Commander of the local Citizens' Defense Corps orders the alert, has the public warning sounded usually short blasts on air horns, power horns or steam whistles or on the wailing sirens—and if the bombers arrive overhead, directs the operation of passive defense. Learn the air raid warning for your city.

FLASH

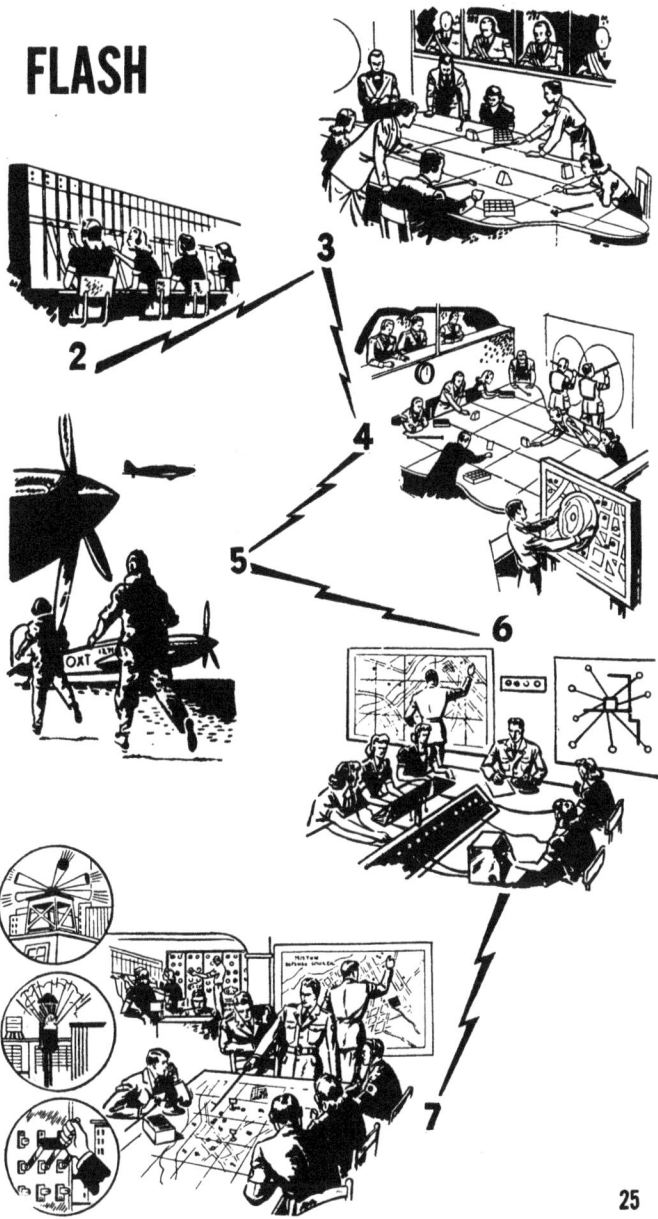

The Refuge Room

WHAT TO DO IN AN AIR RAID

At the yellow warning, if you are not already on duty, you will be summoned to your post and will carry out orders until relieved. However, here are the rules for those who do not have assigned duties when the air raid warning comes. Memorize them carefully so that you can in turn instruct others. Here is what to tell them:

1. If away from home, seek the nearest shelter. Get off the street.

2. If you are driving, first park your car at the curb; be sure all lights are shut off.

3. If you are at home, send the others to the refuge room. This should be a comfortable place with as little window exposure as possible, equipped with drinking water, things to read, toilet facilities, a flashlight, a portable radio, a sturdy table, and food if you like.

4. Turn off all gas stove burners but leave pilot lights, water heaters and furnaces alone. Leave electricity and water on. Fill some large containers or a bathtub with water.

5. Check up on blackout arrangements. Don't let a crack of light show to the outside.

6. See that everyone's eyeglasses and dentures are in the refuge room. There should be additional warm garments for everyone, too.

7. Keep out of line of windows. Fragments and glass splinters cause most casualties.

8. If bombs fall nearby, get under a heavy table, an overturned davenport.

9. Don't rush out when the "all clear" signal sounds. Maintain the blackout. The Raiders may return.

10. Otherwise, keep cool; be sensible and set an example to others.

FIRE DEFENSE

It will be very difficult to fight a magnesium bomb unless some work is done before the attack

All furniture trunks and junk of all kinds should be removed from attic or top floor!

Roof beams joists and studs can be treated to resist flame — giving more time to reach the bomb.

Paint does no good! A heavy coat of ordinary whitewash helps some

HOW THE MAGNESIUM BOMB WORKS

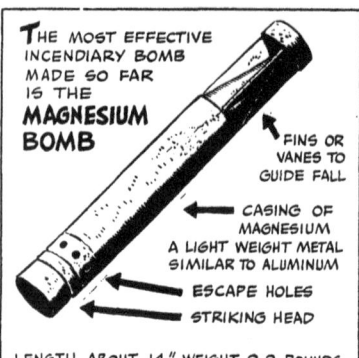

The most effective incendiary bomb made so far is the **MAGNESIUM BOMB**

← FINS OR VANES TO GUIDE FALL
← CASING OF MAGNESIUM A LIGHT WEIGHT METAL SIMILAR TO ALUMINUM
← ESCAPE HOLES
← STRIKING HEAD

LENGTH, ABOUT 14" WEIGHT, 2.2 POUNDS

A large bomber can carry 1000 such bombs!

They are usually released 20 to 50 at a time, spread like shot before striking.

Dropped from a height of 20,000 feet, they develop enough force to penetrate an average roof...

...thus, they usually start burning in a top story or attic

The thermite filling of iron oxide and finely divided aluminum is then ignited and develops a fierce heat of **OVER 4500 DEGREES!**

The flame roars out of the escape holes.

The magnesium casing catches fire, with a sputtering action...

...flaming molten metal is thrown about and surrounding inflammable material catches fire

If not quickly quenched, the bomb will burn through the floor, setting additional fires on the floor below...

BUT, WITH PROMPT ACTION AND SIMPLE TOOLS, A MAGNESIUM BOMB CAN BE QUENCHED!

CONTROLLING WITH SAND

Approach the bomb in a crouching or crawling position. Place the sand bucket, upset, to allow a full-arm swing toward the bomb

Try to cover the bomb with dry sand, to confine it's action, so that you can get near enough to scoop it up on the shovel

When the bomb is under fair control, scoop it up on the shovel, first righting the bucket, but leaving some sand in the bottom...

...if the bomb can be dropped from a window to some place where it can burn out without harm — **GET RID OF IT THAT WAY!**

...otherwise, put it in the bucket on top of sand, cover it with more sand...

...then, holding the bucket on the shovel, carry it out of the house...

ABOUT FIRE EXTINGUISHERS

Many houses and public buildings have fire extinguishers. They will be as useful as ever in putting out fires caused by an incendiary bomb. For putting out the bomb itself, the extinguisher may not be suitable.

Read the label. If it says that the contents include CARBON TETRACHLORIDE, it cannot under any circumstances be used on a magnesium bomb. It is not only ineffective, it may cause dangerous gas to be generated. After the bomb is burnt out, use it on any remaining fire.

All water-type extinguishers are suitable. If the label says SODA-ACID, that's simply a means of creating pressure in the extinguisher. Turn it upside down, use it. You can get a spray effect by putting the thumb over the nozzle, use the jet on surrounding fires. However, *one extinguisher is not enough to burn out a magnesium bomb.* And you cannot refill the extinguisher.

It is best to have sand or pump-bucket equipment handy, use them on the bomb, and save the extinguishers for resulting fires.

A foam extinguisher will also help to control a bomb, but one extinguisher load will not finish the job.

See that the extinguishers you know about are ready for use.

CHEMICAL WARFARE AGENTS
REFERENCE AND TRAINING CHART

LEGEND: HOSPITAL CASE | FIRST AID STATION | LUNG PROTECTION NEEDED | COMPLETE PROTECTION NEEDED

The importance of proper first aid for gas victims cannot be overemphasized. The following are general rules which apply in all cases.

A. Act promptly and quietly; be calm.
B. Put a gas mask on the patient if gas is still present or, if he has a mask on, check to see that his is properly adjusted. If a mask is not available, wet a handkerchief or other cloth and have him breathe through it.
C. Keep the patient at absolute rest; loosen clothing to facilitate breathing.
D. Remove the patient to a gas-free place as soon as possible.
E. Summon medical aid promptly; if possible, send the victim to a hospital.
F. Do not permit the patient to smoke, as this causes coughing and, hence, exertion.

CLASS	NAMES AND SYMBOLS	FORM	ODOR	PERSISTENCE	TACTICAL CLASS	PROTECTION	FIRST AID (After removal from gassed area)	PHYSIOLOGICAL EFFECT
VESICANTS	MUSTARD $S(CH_2CH_2)_2Cl_2$ H-2(M)(HT), SULFIDE	LIQUID AND VAPOR	Garlic, Horseradish, Mustard	One day to one week. Longer if dry or cold.			Undress; remove liquid mustard with protective ointment, Bleach paste, or kerosene; bathe; wash eyes and nose with soda solution.	Delayed effect. Burns skin or membrane. Inflammatory respiratory tract; leading to pneumonia. Eye irritation, conjunctivitis.
VESICANTS	LEWISITE $ClCH:CH\cdot AsCl_2$ CHLORVINYL-2-DICHLORARSINE	LIQUID AND VAPOR	Flypaper, musty	One day to one week. Longer if dry or cold.			Undress; remove liquid Lewisite with hydrogen peroxide, lye in glycerine, or kerosene; bathe; wash eyes and nose with soda. Rest—Doctor.	Burning or irritation of eyes, nasal passages, respiratory tract, skin. Arsenical poison.
LUNG IRRITANTS	CHLORPICRIN CCl_3NO_2 NITROCHLOROFORM	GAS	Ensilage, Acrid	Open 3 hours. Woods 12 hours.			Wash eyes, keep quiet and warm. Do not use bandages.	Causes severe coughing, crying, vomiting.
LUNG IRRITANTS	DIPHOSGENE $ClCOOC\cdot Cl_3$ TRICHLOROMETHYL CHLOROFORMATE	GAS	Musty hay, Green corn	30 minutes.			Keep quiet and warm. Give coffee as a stimulant.	Causes coughing, breathing hurts, eyes water, toxic.
LUNG IRRITANTS	PHOSGENE $COCl_2$ CARBONYL CHLORIDE	GAS	Apple blossoms	10 to 30 minutes.			Keep quiet and warm, bed rest. Coffee as a stimulant. Loosen clothing. No alcohol or cigarettes.	Irritation of lungs, occasional vomiting, tears in eyes, dry and fainting. Occasionally symptoms delayed. Later, collapse, heart failure.
LACRIMATORS	CLORACETOPHENONE $C_6H_5\cdot CO\cdot CH_2Cl$	GAS	Sour fruit	10 minutes.			Wash eyes with cold water or boric acid solution. Do not bandage. Face wind. For skin, sodium sulphite solution.	Makes eyes smart. Shut tightly. Tears flow. Temporary.
LACRIMATORS	BROMBENZYLCYANIDE $C_6H_5\cdot CH\cdot BrCN$	GAS		Several days. (Fresh in winter.)			Wash eyes with boric acid. Do not bandage.	Eyes smart, shut, tears flow. Effect lasts same time. Headache.
STERNUTATORS	ADAMSITE $(C_6H_4)_2\cdot NHAsCl$ DIPHENYLAMINECHLORARSINE	GAS	Dust bombs	10 minutes.			Keep quiet and warm. Loosen clothing. Reassure. Spray mask with soap-epinephrin or sniff bleaching powder. Aspirin for headache.	Causes sneezing, sick depressed feeling, headache.
STERNUTATORS	DIPHENYLCHLORARSINE $(C_6H_5)_2\cdot AsCl$	SMOKE	Shoe Polish	Summer 10 minutes.			Remove to pure air, keep quiet. Sniff chlorine from bleaching powder bottle.	Causes sick feeling and headache.

32

WAR GASES

General Notes.

War "Gases," or chemical agents used to produce casualties, are surprise weapons. As this is written, they have not been used against the British or others trained to protect themselves. They have been used against the Ethiopians and the Chinese.

A gas-tight room suitably located offers fair protection against any probable concentration of war gas in a city. For those whose duties take them into the streets a gas mask offers full protection against all but the "blister gases" (liquid vesicants). To enter areas where mustard or lewisite is present, full protective clothing is needed.

War gases may be dropped in bombs or simple containers and liquid vesicants may also be sprayed by airplanes.

The gas warning is a "percussion sound"—that is, bells, drums, hand rattles, rapidly struck resonant objects of any kind. If the presence of gas is suspected, report to the nearest warden. Do not shout if distant gas alarms are heard. The danger is local and the spreading of an alarm must be left to the wardens.

The notes on the following pages are simply for reference for those who have received instruction in protection against gas. Reading them will not by itself make you an expert in gas defense.

THE GAS-TIGHT ROOM

War gases hug the ground, flow into cellars and basements. Upper floors of a dwelling are away from dangerous concentrations. If all openings and cracks are closed, a room three stories from the ground will offer good protection against war gases.

To stop cracks and small openings, tape of various kinds may be used. A mush made by soaking newspapers in water or patching plaster may be used for caulking larger openings. A piece of wall board, nails and caulking material may be kept handy to cover a window broken by the blast of high explosives.

One door may be used as an entrance by fastening over it a blanket in such a way as to seal it tightly when no one is going in or out. If soaked in oil to close the air spaces, the blanket is more effective.

Store necessary supplies in such a room—food, water, chairs, a battery-operated radio, flashlight and by all means provide some sort of toilet facilities use it as the refuge room.

Allow 20 square feet of floor space for each person who is to occupy an average room with a ceiling nine feet high. This will give enough air to occupy the room 10 hours.

The illustration shows where to stop up cracks, how to hang the blanket at the entrance door.

"Blister Gases" and Decontamination.

Lewisite and mustard "gas" are liquids in the normal state. They give off a dangerous vapor that acts as a war gas and unless chemically neutralized may persist for a week, contaminating the air for a considerable distance down wind.

Full protection against these chemical agents is afforded by gas-proof clothing, covering the wearer from top to toe and tightened at wrists and ankles. The greatest care must be used in undressing after exposure to lewisite or mustard and this is done at personnel decontamination stations, where vesicant casualties are also taken for first aid.

Decontamination of streets, walls, and buildings is effected principally by means of chloride of lime (bleaching powder) freshly mixed with earth and water as a slurry or paste. It must be thoroughly worked into cracks and crevices and the resulting product flushed away. This work is done by the decontamination squads.

The liquid vesicants are very penetrating and ordinary shoes or clothing offer no protection. Do not go into the streets after a gas alarm has been sounded except on direction of the Warden.

RANK DESIGNATION	▲	▲▲	▲▲▲	△	△△	△△△	★	★★	★★★	★★★★
AIR RAID WARDEN	FIRST CLASS	SENIOR OR SECTOR WARDEN	ZONE LEADER	GROUP LEADER	CHIEF WARDEN	STATE WARDEN	NO OTHER RANKS			
AUXILIARY FIREMEN	"	SQUAD LEADER	PLATOON LEADER	COMPANY LEADER	FIRE CHIEF	STATE FIRE COORDINATOR	NO OTHER RANKS			
AUXILIARY POLICEMEN	"	"	"	"	CHIEF OF POLICE	NO OTHER RANKS				
BOMB SQUADS	"	"	NONE	"	"	NO OTHER RANKS				
RESCUE SQUADS	"	"	DEPOT LEADER	"	FIRE CHIEF	NO OTHER RANKS				
MEDICAL FIELD UNITS	"	TEAM LEADER	SQUAD LEADER	UNIT LEADER	CHIEF OF E.M.S.	STATE MEDICAL DIRECTOR				
MEDICAL AUXILIARIES (stretcher teams)	"	" ★	" ★	NO OTHER RANKS	CHIEF WARDEN	NO OTHER RANKS				
NURSES' AIDES	NO RANK DESIGNATIONS									
EMERGENCY FOOD AND HOUSING	FIRST CLASS	UNIT LEADER	DEPOT LEADER	COMPANY LEADER	CHIEF WARDEN	NO OTHER RANKS				
DRIVERS UNITS	"	CONVOY LEADER	"	"	NO OTHER RANKS					
MESSENGERS	"	SENIOR MESSENGER	PLATOON LEADER	"	NO OTHER RANKS					
ROAD REPAIR CREWS	"	CREW LEADER	DEPOT LEADER	"						
DEMOLITION AND CLEAR.	"	"	"	"	CHIEF OF EMER. WORK S.	NO OTHER RANKS				
DECONTAMINATION SQUADS	"	SQUAD LEADER	STATION LEADER	"						
FIRE WATCHERS	"	NO OTHER RANKS								
REPAIR CREWS	"	CREW LEADER	SERVICE LEADER	NONE	CHIEF OF UTILITIES	NO OTHER RANKS				
LOCAL STAFF	"	AS REQUIRED		STAFF UNIT LEADER	CONTROLLER	COMMANDER	COORDINATOR	NO OTHER RANKS		
STATE STAFF	"	AS REQUIRED			AS DESIGNATED	AS DESIGNATED	ASST. COORDINATOR	COORDINATOR	NO OTHER RANKS	
U.S. STAFF	"	AS REQUIRED				AS DESIGNATED	AS DESIGNATED	AS DESIGNATED	REGION DIRECTOR PRINCIPAL ASST'S	U.S. DIRECTOR
EQUIVALENT ARMY TERM	PVT. 1st CLASS	NON-COMM. OFF.	LIEUTENANT	CAPTAIN	MAJOR	COLONEL	BRIG. GEN.	MAJ. GEN.	LIEUT. GEN.	GENERAL

★ASSIGNED BY RED CROSS TO CHIEF OF EMERGENCY MEDICAL SERVICE.

CITIZENS' DEFENSE CORPS

The team of trained civilian services organized to operate the passive defense is known as the Citizens' Defense Corps. It includes regular forces of the city—police, firemen, welfare workers, sanitation men—as well as volunteers. It operates as a unit under the local Defense Coordinator.

Staff.

The Citizens' Defense Corps is headed by a Commander assisted by a staff. His second in command is the Executive Officer. There are others who operate the control center and the communications, account for personnel and property and assign transportation. The Chiefs of the Fire and Police Departments assist him in the passive defense. There is a Chief Air Raid Warden, a Chief of Emergency Medical Services, and others who control groups of the enrolled volunteers. Learn the organization of the Citizens' Defense Corps in your community.

Enrolled Volunteer Services of The Citizens' Defense Corps.

Air Raid Wardens are in complete charge of a sector containing the homes of about 500 people. To them the warden is the embodiment of all Civilian Defense.

Auxiliary Firemen assist the regular fire-fighting forces.

Auxiliary Policemen assist the police department in enforcing blackout restrictions, in traffic control, and in guard duties.

 Bomb Squads are specially trained squads of police to handle and dispose of time bombs and duds.

 Rescue Squads are trained crews of about 10 men each with special equipment to rescue the injured from debris.

 Medical Forces consist of first-aid parties and stretcher squads and personnel at casualty clearing stations. Members of these forces are doctors, trained nurses, and assistants.

 Nurses' Aides assist nurses. They have special Red Cross Training.

 Emergency Food and Housing Corps members provide welfare services to the needy and homeless.

 Drivers Units consist of emergency drivers of vehicles used by the Civilian Defense services.

 Messengers carry supplies, dispatches, and messages wherever needed.

 Road Repair Crews restore normal flow of traffic as quickly as possible. Utility repair men work with these crews and with demolition squads.

 Demolition and Clearance Crews remove rubble, fill bomb craters, and remove unsafe walls or parts of buildings.

 Decontamination squad members are specially trained to treat clothing and equipment as well as streets and walls contaminated by war gas.

 Fire Watchers must spot and combat incendiary bombs.

A MANUAL OF DRILL
for the
CITIZENS' DEFENSE CORPS

Adapted from the Basic Field Manual of the United States Army

Basic drill is required of a volunteer for award of the insigne. Drill for units of the Citizens' Defense Corps, moreover, is recommended as it helps to coordinate the work of individuals under a single command. The purposes of drill are:

1 To enable a leader to move his unit from one place to another in an orderly manner.

2 To aid in disciplinary training by instilling habits of precision and response to the leader's orders.

3 To provide a means, through ceremonies, of enhancing the morale; develop a spirit of cohesion; and give an interesting spectacle to the public.

4 To give leaders practical training in commanding volunteers.

Drills should be frequent, intensive, and of short duration.

General.

A normal squad of volunteers contains 12 men or 12 women, all of one service. It consists of a leader, an assistant leader, and other personnel. As far as practicable, the squad is kept intact. The usual formation of the squad is a single rank or single file. This permits variations in the number of men composing the squad.

To Form the Squad.

The command is; FALL IN. At the command FALL IN the squad forms in line as shown. Squad leader on the squad's extreme right, assistant leader on the squad's extreme left.

To secure uniformity, the tallest leader is put in charge of the first squad, the second tallest in charge of the second squad, etc. Assistant

Fig. I—A Squad in Line

leaders are similarly arranged. Other volunteers are placed according to height beginning with the tallest being placed next to the leader.

On falling in, each man except the one on the left extends his left arm laterally at shoulder height, palm of the hand down, fingers extended and joined. Each man, except the one on the right, turns his head and eyes to the right and places himself in line so that his right shoulder touches lightly the tips of the fingers of the man on his right. As soon as proper intervals have been obtained, each man comes to attention, drops his arm smartly to his side and turns his head to

Fig. II—A Volunteer at Attention

the front, heels are together, feet forming a right angle; knees are straight without stiffness, hips level and drawn back slightly, body erect and resting equally on hips, chest lifted and arched, shoulders square and falling equally. Arms hang straight down without stiffness with the back of the hands out, fingers held naturally. Head erect and squarely to the front, chin drawn in so that the axis of the head and neck is vertical, eyes straight to the front. The weight of the body rests equally on the heels and the balls of the feet. In assuming the position of attention the heels are brought together smartly and audibly.

(Leaders and assistant leaders will be appointed under authority defined by the Chief of the Service of which the squad forms a part.

To Form at Close Intervals.

The commands are: At Close Interval, FALL IN. At the command FALL IN, the volunteers fall in as described above, except that close intervals are obtained by placing the left hands on the hips. In this position the heel of the palm of the hand rests on the hip, the fingers and thumb are extended and joined, and the elbow is in the plane of the body.

Fig. III—A Volunteer Falling in at Close Interval

To Aline the Squad.

If in line, the commands are: Dress Right, DRESS, Ready, Front. At the command DRESS, each man except the one on the left extends his left arm (or if at close interval, places his left hand upon his hip), and all aline themselves to the right. The instructor places himself on the right flank one pace from and in prolongation of the line and facing down the line. From this position he verifies the alinement of the men, ordering individual men to move forward or back as is necessary. Having checked the alinement, he faces to the right in marching and moves three paces forward, halts, faces to the left and commands: Ready, FRONT. At the command FRONT, arms are dropped quietly and smartly to the sides and heads turned to the front.

Rests.

Being at a halt the commands are: FALL OUT, REST, AT EASE, and PARADE REST.

At the command FALL OUT, volunteers leave the ranks but are required to remain in the immediate vicinity.

At the command REST, one foot is kept in place. Silence and immobility are not required.

At the command AT EASE the right foot is

kept in place. Silence but not immobility is required.

At the command of execution **REST** of Parade **REST**, move the left foot smartly 12 inches to the left of the right foot keeping the legs straight so that the weight of the body rests equally on both feet. At the same time, clasp the hands behind the back, palms to the rear, thumb and fingers of the right hand clasping the left thumb without constraint; preserving silence and immobility.

Being at any of the rests except **FALL OUT**, to resume the position of Attention, the commands are Squad (or other unit being commanded) **ATTENTION**. At the command **ATTENTION** take that position in your squad.

Eyes right (left).

The commands are: Eyes (Preliminary Command), **RIGHT** (Command of Execution) (LEFT) Ready **FRONT!** At the command **RIGHT**, each man turns his head and eyes to the right. At the command **FRONT** the head and eyes are turned to the front.

Facings.

(*All Facings are executed at the halt.*)

To the flank.—The commands are Right (Left) FACE. At the command FACE, slightly raise the left heel and the right toe: Face to the right, turning on the right heel, assisted by a slight pressure on the ball of the left foot. Next, place the left foot beside the right. Exercise Left FACE on the left heel in a corresponding manner.

To the rear.—The commands are: About FACE. At the command FACE, carry the toe of the right foot a half-foot length to the rear and slightly to the left of the left heel without changing

Fig. IV—Executing Right FACE

the position of the left foot; weight of the body mainly on the heel of the left foot; right leg straight without stiffness. (TWO) Face to the rear turning to the right on the left heel and on the ball of the right foot, place the right heel beside the left.

Steps and Marchings.

All steps and marchings executed from the halt, except right step, begin with the left foot.

Quick Time: Being at a halt, to march forward in quick time, the commands are: Forward MARCH. At the command Forward, shift the weight of the body to the right leg without perceptible movement. At the command MARCH, step off smartly with the left foot and continue the march with steps taken straight forward without stiffness or exaggeration of movements. Swing the arms easily in their natural arcs, 6 inches to the front and 3 inches to the rear of the body. To halt when marching in quick time, the commands are: Squad HALT. At the command HALT, given as either foot strikes the ground, execute the halt in two counts by advancing and planting the other foot and then bringing up the foot in rear.

To Mark Time the commands are; Mark-Time, MARCH.

Being in march at the command MARCH, given as either foot strikes the ground, advance and plant the other foot, bring up the foot in rear, placing it so that both heels are on line and continue the cadence by alternately raising and planting each foot. The feet are raised 2 inches from the ground.

Being at a halt, at the command MARCH, raise and plant first the left then the right as prescribed above.

The halt is executed from mark time as from quick time.

Half Step.—The commands are: Half Step MARCH. At the command MARCH, take steps of 15 inches in quick time. To resume the full step from the half step or mark time the commands are: Forward MARCH.

Side Step.—Being at a halt the commands are: Right (Left) Step MARCH. At the command MARCH, carry the right foot 12 inches to the right, place the left foot beside the right, left knee straight. Continue the cadence of quick time. (The side step is executed in quick time from the halt and for short distances only.)

Back Step.—Being at a halt the commands are, Backward MARCH. At the command MARCH, take steps, beginning with the left foot, 15 inches straight to the rear.

To March to the Flank.—Being in march the commands are: By The Right (Left) Flank—MARCH. At the command MARCH, given as the right (left) foot strikes the ground, advance and plant the left (right) foot, then face to the right (left) in marching and step off in the new direction.

Oblique March.—Being in march the commands are Right (Left) Oblique—MARCH. At the command MARCH, given as the right (left) foot strikes the ground, advance and plant the left (right) foot, then face to the right (left) oblique in marching and step off in the new direction.

To resume the original direction, the commands are—Forward, MARCH. At the command MARCH each individual faces half left (right) in marching then moves straight to the front.

Change Step.—The commands are Change Step, MARCH. Being in march at quick time, at the command MARCH, given as the right foot strikes the ground, advance and plant the left foot, plant the toe of the right foot near the heel of the left and step off with the left foot. (Execute the change on the right foot similarly, the command MARCH being given as the left foot strikes the ground.)

To the Rear.—To face to the rear in marching, being in march, the commands are: To The Rear, MARCH. At the command MARCH, given as the right foot strikes the ground, advance and plant the left foot, turn to the right about on the balls of both feet and immediately step off with the left foot.

Other Marchings.—March other than at Attention. The commands are: Route Step, MARCH or At Ease, MARCH. Route Step MARCH, at the command MARCH Volunteers are not required to march at attention or to maintain silence. At Ease, MARCH is the same as Route Step, MARCH, except that Volunteers will maintain silence.

Dismissing the Squad.—The unit being at a halt the leader calls the unit to attention, if they are not at attention, from a point six paces in front of the center of the unit. He then will give the command—DISMISSED. Volunteers are then free to go and do as they please until the next regularly scheduled drill period.

Forming the Platoon.

To form the platoon, which consists of 3 squads—the command, FALL IN will be given by the senior leader facing the area on which he wishes the platoon to form. At this command the unit will form facing the leader with its center 6 paces to his front in 3 parallel lines (each of these lines constitutes a squad). (Should there be insufficient men to form 3 complete squads, skeleton squads of as near equal number as possible will be formed in 3 ranks, squad leaders placing themselves directly behind one another.)

Fig. V.—A Platoon in Column of Squads

From this formation the unit can march; forward, to the right, or to the left.

Platoon Movements.

At the command: Forward MARCH, each man steps off with his left foot directly to his own front preserving his relative position and so regulates his step that the ranks remain parallel to his original front.

At the command: Right (Left) FACE Forward MARCH, the unit executes a right face on the heel of the right foot and ball of the left foot at the word FACE and at the word MARCH they step off with their left foot as in moving to the front. (Left face is performed by turning on the heel of the left foot and the ball of the right foot.) In the movements to the right or left the commander of the unit takes a position three paces in front of the left file of his command, at double time if necessary.

Being in a column to change direction the commands are—Column Right (Left) MARCH. At the command MARCH, given as the right (left) foot strikes the ground the first man of the leading element on the right (left) advances one step and then steps off in the new direction using half steps until the men to his left (right) are abreast of him. Full step is then resumed.

Close Interval—Normal Interval.—Being in column of threes at normal interval between squads to March or form at Close Interval, the commands are: Close, MARCH. At the command MARCH, the squads close to the center by obliquing until the interval between men is 4 inches. The center squad take up the half step until the dress has been regained.

If this movement is executed from the halt, the squads close toward the center by executing Right or Left Step until 4-inch intervals are reached.

Being in column of threes at close interval between squads to March or form at Normal Interval, the commands are: Extend, MARCH. At the command MARCH, the squads open to the right and left from the center by obliquing until the normal interval is regained.

If this movement is executed from the halt, the squads Right or Left Step until normal interval is regained.

Change Direction.—Being in column of threes to change direction, the commands are: Column Right (Left) MARCH. The right flank man of the leading rank is the pivot. At the command MARCH, given as the right foot strikes the ground, the right flank man of the leading rank faces to the right in marching and takes up the half step until the other men of his rank are abreast of him, then he resumes the full step. The other men of the leading rank oblique to the right in marching without changing interval, place themselves abreast of the pivot man, and conform to his step. The ranks in rear of the leading rank execute the movement on the same ground and in the same manner as the leading rank.

Fig. VI
Forming the Citizens' Defense Corps for Parade

(Services will form and move as platoons)

- ● Mayor, Defense Coordinator and Dignitaries.
- ☐ Commander, C. D. C.
- ▭ Staff.
- ▭ Messengers.
- ▭ Drivers.
- ☐ Fire Department Chief.
- ▭ Auxiliary Firemen.
- ▭ Rescue Squads.
- ☐ Police Department Chief.
- ▭ Auxiliary Police.
- ▭ Bomb Squads.
- ☐ Colors.
- ☐ Warden Service Chief.
- ▭ Air Raid Wardens.
- ▭ Fire Watchers.
- ▭ Emergency Food Housing Units.
- ☐ Medical Service Chief.
- ▭ Medical Field Units.
- ▭ Nurses' Aides Corps.
- ☐ Public Works Service Chief.
- ▭ Demolition and Clearance Crews.
- ▭ Road Repair Squads.
- ▭ Decontamination Corps.

www.ingramcontent.com/pod-product-compliance
Ingram Content Group UK Ltd.
Pitfield, Milton Keynes, MK11 3LW, UK
UKHW021323180426
11947UKWH00017B/1398